ADAM & EVE

Adapted by Tess Fries
Illustrated by Cheryl Mendenhall

Art Directed by Shannon Osborne Thompson

SPIRIT PRESS and DALMATIAN PRESS are trademarks of
Dalmatian Press, LLC, Franklin, Tennessee 37067.
No part of this book may be reproduced or copied in any form
without the written permission of Dalmatian Press.

ISBN: 1-40370-967-X
11449-0804

Printed in the U.S.A.

04 05 06 07 LBM 10 9 8 7 6 5 4 3 2 1

Long ago when God made the world and all that was in it, He created the very first man. The man's name was Adam. God made Adam from the dust of the ground, and then He breathed life into him.

God put Adam in a wonderful garden named Eden. There were all kinds of plants, animals and trees in the garden. The trees were beautiful. Some trees had wonderful fruit that Adam could eat and enjoy.

In the middle of the garden grew the Tree of Knowledge of Good and Evil.

God told Adam, "You may eat the fruit from every tree in the garden, except from the Tree of Knowledge of Good and Evil. The day that you eat from that tree — you will die."

Adam spent time in the garden tending the plants for God. It was joyful work and a happy life for Adam.

One day, God brought all the marvelous creatures He had made to Adam and gave him the job of naming them. Adam named the cattle, the frogs, the raven and the lions. Large and small, furry and feathered, Adam gave each one a name.

After all of the animals were named, God looked at Adam and said, "It is not good for man to be alone." He caused Adam to fall into a very deep sleep. God then took one of Adam's ribs and from it made the first woman. Her name was Eve and she became Adam's wife.

They enjoyed living in the garden among the friendly animals and the beautiful plants. But the best part was being near God, and walking and talking with Him in the garden.

Now, the serpent was a very deceptive creature in the garden. One day he came to Eve and said, "You will not die if you eat the fruit from the Tree of Knowledge of Good and Evil. God knows that if you eat it, you will become a god like He is."

Eve looked at the fruit. It was beautiful and looked like it would taste delicious. Eve decided to believe the serpent instead of listening to God. She took the fruit and ate it. She gave some to Adam — and he ate it, too.

At once, Adam and Eve knew they had done something terribly wrong! They had disobeyed God. They were ashamed and afraid.

Later, they heard God's voice as He walked through the garden, so they hid. "Adam, where are you?" God asked. Adam said, "I heard your voice, and I was afraid." God asked Adam if he had eaten the forbidden fruit. Adam replied, "Eve gave me the fruit, and I ate it."

God was not happy that Adam and Eve had disobeyed Him and were deceived by the serpent. He said to the serpent, "Because of this, you will have to crawl on your belly forever."

Then God told
Adam and Eve,
"Because you
have eaten the
forbidden fruit,
you must leave
the garden," and
He drove them
out of the
Garden of Eden.

Cherubim were
placed at the
entrance of the
garden to
guard it.

Adam and Eve began their new lives outside the garden. They had to make a home among the rocks and trees. They worked hard to grow food among the thistles and weeds. But worst of all, they could no longer walk with God.

Because they had disobeyed God, Adam and Eve — and everyone born after them — would die as God had said. Because God's love is so great, He sent His Son to take the punishment for all our sins, so that we can have eternal life.

"The LORD God took the man and put
him in the Garden of Eden to
work it and take care of it."
Genesis 2:15
(NIV)